TIKTOK

YOUR GUIDE TO
THE BIGGEST STARS
OF TIKTOK

DEAN

First published in Great Britain 2021 by Dean, part of Farshore
An imprint of HarperCollins*Publishers*
1 London Bridge Street, London SE1 9GF
www.farshore.co.uk

HarperCollins*Publishers*
1st Floor, Watermarque Building, Ringsend Road
Dublin 4, Ireland

Written by Samantha Wood and Suzie Brearley
Illustrated by Irina Kamyshanskaya
Designed by Ian Pollard

This book is an original creation by Farshore
100% Unofficial: TikTok © 2021 Farshore

ISBN 978 0 7555 0271 4
Printed in Italy
1

ONLINE SAFETY FOR YOUNGER FANS

Spending time online is great fun! Here are a few simple rules to help younger fans
stay safe and keep the internet a great place to spend time:

- Never give out your real name - don't use it as your username.
- Never give out any of your personal details.
- Never tell anybody which school you go to or how old you are.
- Never tell anybody your password except a parent or a guardian.
- Be aware that you must be 13 or over to create an account on many sites. Always
check the site policy and ask a parent or guardian for permission before registering.
- Always tell a parent or guardian if something is worrying you.

Stay safe online. Farshore is not responsible for content hosted by third parties.

Farshore takes its responsibility to the planet and its inhabitants very seriously.
We aim to use papers from well-managed forests run by responsible suppliers.

100% UNOFFICIAL

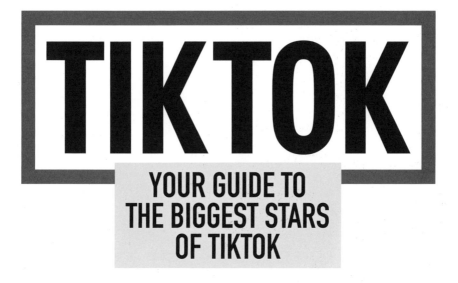

TIKTOK

YOUR GUIDE TO THE BIGGEST STARS OF TIKTOK

Samantha Wood

@addisonre

@maxandharveyofficial

@itsjojosiwa

@jacobsartorius

@ameliagething

@babyariel

@joshrichards

@sofiawylie

@zachking

@charlidamelio

@dixiedamelio

@twitchtok7

4

CONTENTS

MAGIC • DANCE • SING • ACT • PRANKS • FASHION • BEAUTY

TOK TILL YOU DROP

STAY SAFE ONLINE

Staying safe is the most important part of being online

S taying safe online is super important. Make sure you ask an adult before venturing onto any new online platform. And before you read through the pages of this super-awesome guide about all things TikTok, here are some guidelines for keeping safe.

TIKTOK'S MINIMUM AGE IS 13

This means you can't set up your profile until you are 13 or older. If you are old enough to be online, here are some top tips.

ASK FOR PERMISSION

Make sure you ask an adult for permission to sign up to any social media profiles. They will help you stay safe!

TELL SOMEONE

If anything at all makes you feel uncomfortable make sure you tell an adult immediately! Online fun should be exactly that, fun!

NEVER GIVE OUT YOUR PERSONAL INFORMATION

There are lots of people online pretending to be other people. Never give out your name, address or what school you go to, even if the person seems normal.

SET YOUR PRIVACY SETTINGS

One of the easiest ways to protect your posts is to set your privacy settings. Make sure you have your profile set up so that only people YOU choose can see your posts.

ONLINE FUN SHOULD BE EXACTLY THAT, FUN!

NEVER GIVE OUT YOUR PASSWORD

Protect your password from anyone online! It's too easy for someone to log in and pretend to be you so it's important never to share your password.

THINK BEFORE YOU POST

Once you post something online, anyone can screenshot it and share it so make sure you would be happy for your parents, teachers, friends, family, or anyone else to see what you post!

BLOCK ANYTHING THAT MAKES YOU FEEL UNCOMFORTABLE

It doesn't matter what it is, whether it's a comment or a post, anything that makes you feel uncomfortable should be blocked immediately. Make sure you tell an adult about anything that makes you feel like this.

IT'S NOT REAL LIFE

Remember that posting online is not real life. Most people only post the highlights so if you are looking at something online that makes you feel low, take a screen break and try not to compare yourself.

TAKING A BREAK IS GOOD FOR YOU!

REMEMBER TO TAKE BREAKS

Taking a break from the internet is great for your mental health! Try to have at least a couple of hours a day when you are intentionally offline.

BE RESPECTFUL

It's easier to make a comment online than it is in real life, which can lead to online bullying. All creators are working hard to make their content as fun as possible. Make sure you treat other people the way you would like to be treated!

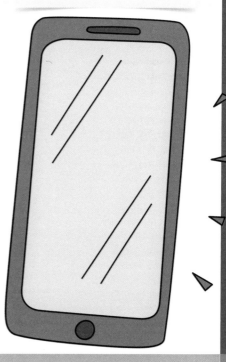

TIKTOK'S
TIMELINE

Just like when you were delivered by the stork, TikTok had to come from somewhere

2014 **2015** **2016**

TikTok is a global phenomenon and if you don't have the app that creates short music, lip-sync, dance and talent vids we bet you know someone who does. But did you know, it hasn't been around for long. And did you also know that some of the biggest TikTok creators were *already* huge on the app that came before? No? Well, buckle up for a history lesson.

● **Aug 2014**
The musical.ly app (founded by long-term pals **Alex Zhu** and **Luyu Yang**) is launched in Shanghai. It allows users to upload short lip-sync videos.

● **July 2015**
musical.ly becomes the most downloaded free app in over 30 countries including the UK, USA, Japan and Brazil.

● **June 2016**
musical.ly has over 90 million users worldwide. These include **Jacob Sartorius**, **Baby Ariel** and **Amelia Gething** who you may have heard of.

● **Sept 2016**
A Chinese tech company called ByteDance launch lip-syncing app Douyin, attracting 100 million users in China and Thailand in a year.

Douyin was developed in 200 days!

JACOB SARTORIUS

BABY ARIEL

Sept 2017
ByteDance launch an early version of TikTok to the international market.

TikTok is now a worldwide app, excluding China. China still has their version Douyin to this day.

Aug 2018
ByteDance merges Douyin with musical.ly creating the TikTok we all know and love.

2019
The Hype House is launched in LA – an exclusive group of TikTok creators who hang out (and sometimes live) together.

TikTok was downloaded 113 million times in Feb 2020 alone!

March 2020
Charli D'Amelio overtakes **Loren Gray** as the most followed TikTok creator.

2017

2018

2019

2020

Nov 2017
ByteDance spend approximately ONE BILLION DOLLARS on buying musical.ly.

Sept 2018
TikTok already surpasses Facebook, Instagram, YouTube and Snapchat in monthly downloads.

TikTok becomes the most downloaded app on the Apple Store!

Feb 2019
TikTok user **Montero Hill** (AKA **Lil Nas X**) uploads his meme 'Old Town Road' which goes viral. He gets a record deal and the song becomes (at the time) the longest running number-one hit on the Billboard Hot 100.

LIL NAS X

TikTok now has more than 800 million users worldwide!

LOREN GRAY

10 THINGS
that make TikTok tick

There's loads more but we've only got two pages

1 IT MAKES YOU SMILE

Although music is at the core of most TikToks, there's heaps of things to turn a frown upside down. From fails to animal LOLs, it's also the place to go for edgy, contemporary comedy. In fact, the most viewed, liked and likely-to-go-viral vids are proven to be the ones that make us snort.

2 IT BRINGS PEOPLE TOGETHER

You know that friend you haven't seen in ages because she moved to another country? Or your cousin that you haven't been able to visit due to social distancing? They're there in your pocket at all times. TikTok brings people together and allows us to feel close to them, even when we're not.

3 YOU CAN UNLEASH YOUR CREATIVITY

Here you can be creative in whatever way YOU want. Whether it's dance, make-up, cooking, magic, pranks or showing off your pet rat's backflips, TikTok is a platform packed with talent and is a great way of showcasing your 100% totally unique skillset.

4 YOU CAN CHANGE THE WORLD

Whatever you're really passionate about, the change you really want to see happen, the movement you believe in - it's all possible when people join forces. TikTok allows us to come together, support each other and re-write the rules.

to all y'all that are becoming more environmental conscious 🌎

5 IT CHALLENGES YOU

Whether that's to nail the latest dance moves or get your dog agile enough to jump yet another layer of loo roll, TikTok is always pushing us to try harder.

6 YOU DON'T NEED A FILTER

Wouldn't it be nice to be seen - and liked - exactly the way you are? Well, that's the joy of TikTok. It rejects the highly polished filters of other social media platforms in favour of showing real people as they are IRL. No filter.

7 IT GETS YOU MOVING

All those dance and fitness challenges that TikTok keep chucking at us are the best incentive to move our bodies. Dancing, jumping, planking, climbing - it's basically a fitness plan, no gym membership required.

8 IT'S GLOBAL

That talent that never makes it any further than the four walls of a bedroom can now be seen by people on the other side of the world. Creators can be good at anything and it has the potential to open doors, shape your future and be celebrated on a global scale.

9 YOUR VIBE ATTRACTS YOUR TRIBE

Whatever you might be into - gaming, cosplay, fitness, make-up, arachnids - there'll be something on TikTok that grabs your attention. The app's 'For You' section uses a clever algorithm to help users find 'their' tribe, meaning you'll never feel like the odd one out.

10 IT CELEBRATES EVERYONE

musical.ly, the app that came before TikTok, was synonymous with teenagers but now more adult creators are getting involved. It embraces everyone, from everywhere, with any ability. Which is the way life should be, quite frankly.

THE BEST OF
MUSICAL.LY

When musical.ly became TikTok it came with some already established superstars

In the time before TikTok there was musical.ly and many TikTok creators began their journey to stratospheric stardom on musical.ly. Do you recognise these famous names?

LOREN GRAY

There she is, the Queen of TikTok – before Charli D'Amelio danced into her 'most followed creator' spot. But before being Top of the Toks, Loren amassed a huge following by lip-syncing on musical.ly. In fact, she's been so popular since 2015, she was one of the first social media stars to make a living out of videos.

JACOB SARTORIUS

Jacob is a perfect example of how messing about with social media can completely change your life. He started uploading lip-syncing videos to musical.ly, was tipped to be 'the next Justin Bieber' and built-up a following of more than 16 million – who then followed him fanatically to TikTok.

BABY ARIEL

Ariel Martin once said that the secret to making a top musical.ly video was having good lighting. Well, her lighting must be next level as she was one of the biggest stars on the lip-syncing app and is still in the top ten most popular TikTok creators.

KRISTEN HANCHER

Years before she was known for her extensive wig collection on TikTok (srsly, how many has she got?), Canadian born Kristen was known for her dancing, singing and acting skills on musical.ly, earning her a cool 15 million or so followers.

MAX AND HARVEY

Identical twins Max and Harvey earned a loyal fanbase by lip-syncing to Shawn Mendes and Avicii on musical.ly before creating their own original content. After success on the app – and before TikTok – they released their debut single *One More Day In Love*.

CAMERON DALLAS

Cameron was being described as an 'internet sensation' long before TikTok became a thing. His seriously pretty face meant he was always going to be popular but he has now become better known for his comedic skills than for his musical ones.

AMELIA GETHING

Comedy has always been this Brit's first love and Amelia used her platform on musical.ly to bring humour to her lip-syncs. She's still serving up the LOLs on TikTok, and that's when she's not writing and recording her own televised comedy show!

MACKENZIE ZIEGLER

You might remember Mackenzie – and her older sister Maddie – from the show *Dance Moms* where they first became a household name. She was then hugely popular on musical.ly, released a single and now keeps busy entertaining her 19.6m TikTok followers.

@charlidamelio

CHARLI D'AMELIO

All rise for the Queen of TikTok

I f you're a fan of Charli D'Amelio's dance and lip-syncing videos then we hate to break it to you, but you haven't discovered something new. The teenager is currently the platform's most popular creator (after pinching Loren Gray's crown, soz Loz) and in less than a year amassed about one and a half times *more* followers than the amount of people who live in the entire UK. Which, in case you're wondering, is a lot.

TikTok
100m
followers

GETTING LIPPY

Charli got her break in 2019 when she uploaded her first video to TikTok of her and a friend lip-syncing to *Hoes Mad* by Famous Dex.

DANCE MAGIC, DANCE

Unsurprisingly those moves didn't come overnight – she's been taking dance lessons since the age of three and competing in competitions since she was five.

Charli's friendly, happy personality helped her take the top TikTok spot!

LOVE BEFORE LOCKDOWN

At the start of 2020, Charli dated fellow TikTok star Chase Hudson for four months. Sadly it wasn't the fairytale ending we were all looking for and ended in a bitter Twitter fall-out.

THE VOICE

Charli recently lent her voice to a little grey mouse called Tinker in the animated film *StarDog and TurboCat*. Squeak!

CHARLIE STATS

DOB: 1st May 2004
Star sign: Taurus
From: Norwalk, Connecticut, USA
TT style: Dancer and lip-syncer
Middle name: Grace
Pet: Chocolate Labrador called Rebel
Fave sweet treat: Dunkin' Donuts

(@zachking)

ZACH KING

You'll never meet anyone more Abraca-fab-ra

Zach King has been making magic videos longer than your little sister's been having hot dinners (mmm, sausages.) He started with the 'digital sleight of hand' stuff on Vine before taking his trickery to TikTok in 2016, absolutely bossing his way to becoming the third most followed creator. But – spoiler alert – Zach isn't some master of witchcraft, he admits that his 'tricks' are actually the result of hours of clever editing.

TikTok
51.8m
followers

PERFECT TIMING

In an interview, Zach said that each of his short videos can take over 24 hours to create, with three to four hours of filming and the rest editing.

RING-A-DING

Zach is happily married having tied the knot with Rachel Holm in 2014. The pair were introduced by Zach's sister at a lip-syncing and dance competition and he proposed the following summer in the field where they had their first snog. Awww.

MUSIC MAN

As well as being a film and editing wizard, Zach is also pretty good at playing the piano and used to practise for three hours a day when he was a kid.

GOING POTTY

In December 2019, Zach uploaded a video of him 'flying' a broomstick which was watched over 2.1 billion times in four days, making it the most viewed video on TikTok ever. It's still unknown whether Harry Potter called asking for his property to be returned.

ZACH STATS

DOB: 4th February 1990
Star sign: Aquarius
From: Portland, Oregon, USA
TT style: Illusionist
Middle name: Michael
Children: Mason and Liam
Fave food: His mum's cooking

TIKTOK BY NUMBERS

We've done the math so you don't have to ...

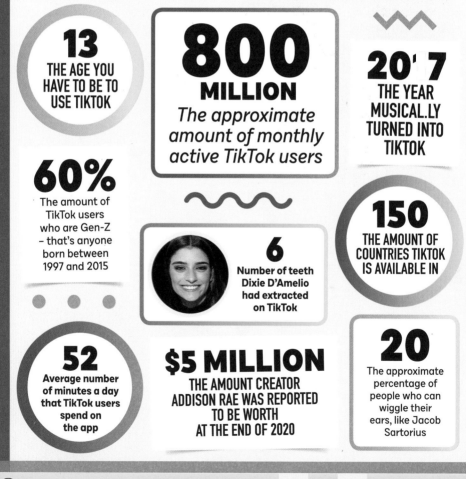

13
THE AGE YOU HAVE TO BE TO USE TIKTOK

800 MILLION
The approximate amount of monthly active TikTok users

20̓7
THE YEAR MUSICAL.LY TURNED INTO TIKTOK

60%
The amount of TikTok users who are Gen-Z – that's anyone born between 1997 and 2015

6
Number of teeth Dixie D'Amelio had extracted on TikTok

150
THE AMOUNT OF COUNTRIES TIKTOK IS AVAILABLE IN

52
Average number of minutes a day that TikTok users spend on the app

$5 MILLION
THE AMOUNT CREATOR ADDISON RAE WAS REPORTED TO BE WORTH AT THE END OF 2020

20
The approximate percentage of people who can wiggle their ears, like Jacob Sartorius

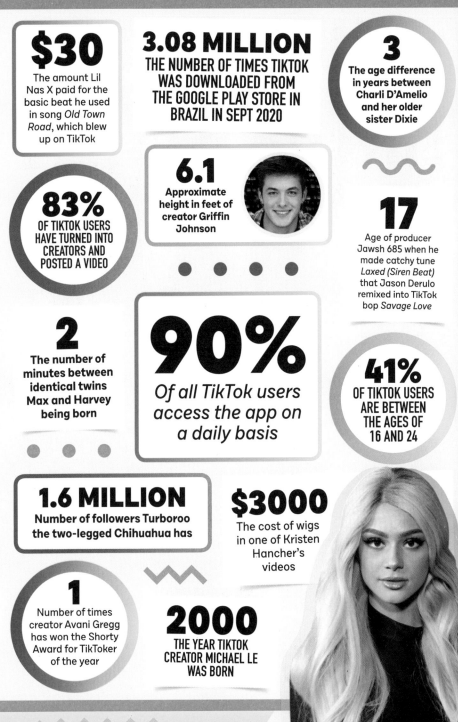

$30
The amount Lil Nas X paid for the basic beat he used in song *Old Town Road*, which blew up on TikTok

3.08 MILLION
THE NUMBER OF TIMES TIKTOK WAS DOWNLOADED FROM THE GOOGLE PLAY STORE IN BRAZIL IN SEPT 2020

3
The age difference in years between Charli D'Amelio and her older sister Dixie

83%
OF TIKTOK USERS HAVE TURNED INTO CREATORS AND POSTED A VIDEO

6.1
Approximate height in feet of creator Griffin Johnson

17
Age of producer Jawsh 685 when he made catchy tune *Laxed (Siren Beat)* that Jason Derulo remixed into TikTok bop *Savage Love*

2
The number of minutes between identical twins Max and Harvey being born

90%
Of all TikTok users access the app on a daily basis

41%
OF TIKTOK USERS ARE BETWEEN THE AGES OF 16 AND 24

1.6 MILLION
Number of followers Turboroo the two-legged Chihuahua has

$3000
The cost of wigs in one of Kristen Hancher's videos

1
Number of times creator Avani Gregg has won the Shorty Award for TikToker of the year

2000
THE YEAR TIKTOK CREATOR MICHAEL LE WAS BORN

What's your TIKTOK STYLE?

Can't decide what content to create? Let us help ...

1 **How would you describe yourself?**
A) Mysterious
B) Energetic
C) Fabulous
D) Adorable

THAT'S ME!

2 **How would your friends describe you?**
A) Unpredictable
B) High-energy
C) Extra
D) Crazy pet person

3 **The weekend is approaching! Plans?**
A) Homework dodging
B) "Alexa, play the latest Dua Lipa album"
C) Perfecting my side ponytail
D) Teaching the cat to Irish-jig

4 **The weekend is over. You actually ended up ...**
A) Copying my BFF's homework
B) Googling the words to all Justin Bieber songs
C) Organising my jumpers in rainbow order
D) Cleaning up cat sick

5 **You're late for school. Why?**
A) We're trying to find the house keys ... which I hid
B) Was waiting to hear my fave song on the radio
C) Couldn't decide which socks matched my outfit
D) The dog was SO close to nailing the Macarena

6 **At a sleepover I'm always the one that ...**
A) Cracks out ghost noises in the dead of night
B) Knows all the words to the playlist
C) Makes the most pyjama effort
D) Sits on the floor with the dog

7 My friends are always begging me to ...

A) Show them my best card trick
B) Have a dance-off
C) Do their hair
D) Bring my dog out

8 My favourite time of year has to be ...

A) Anytime – it's all magical
B) Christmas – time to party!
C) Pride - let's BE the rainbow
D) Spring – baby animals are everything

9 A genie grants you a wish. You wish ...

A) That my annoying little brother would disappear
B) To be more famous than Taylor Swift
C) For a walk-in wardrobe fit for a Carebear
D) That school would shut so I could stay in bed with the cat

You should create ...

MOSTLY A	MOSTLY B	MOSTLY C	MOSTLY D
MAGIC OR PRANKS VIDEOS	**DANCE OR LIP-SYNC TIKTOKS**	**FULL ON FASHION LOOKS**	**CUTE ANIMAL CONTENT**

MAGIC OR PRANKS VIDEOS

Everyone's always looking to you for a laugh and god only knows how you do that thing with the deck of cards (how *do* you do it?) but there's a world of people waiting for you to wow them.

DANCE OR LIP-SYNC TIKTOKS

Oh please, you know *exactly* what content you should be creating on TikTok. The app was made for your dance moves and major lyric knowledge. Jump (slide and shuffle) to the beat please.

FULL ON FASHION LOOKS

Just think, if you didn't start showing the world your crazy talent for turning an everyday outfit into a whirlwind in Disneyland, life would be *so* dull for everyone.

CUTE ANIMAL CONTENT

You're not bothered about being in TikToks, you know that the real star of any show is the one with the fur or feathers. And anyway, it's time you made those furry friends work for their kibbles.

@addisonre

ADDISON RAE

Who knew babysitting could be so lucrative?!

Addison Rae was never planning to be a global superstar. She downloaded TikTok after babysitting for a bunch of younger kids, popped up a video as a bit of a joke and – out of nowhere – it got 93,000 likes. Boom! Stardom pretty much overnight. And her star has been steadily rising ever since. In fact, it's currently a bit brighter than Sirius (the brightest star in the sky, fact fans.)

TikTok
67.7m
followers

TOO COOL FOR SCHOOL

Before moving to LA to be a full-time TikToker and social media megastar she studied sports broadcasting at Louisiana State University.

MEGA LIKES

When she posted a video of her and her mum doing a bop to one of Mariah Carey's songs, it grabbed the attention of Mariah herself. The megastar 'liked' the video, making it go viral.

STRANGE DREAMS

One of her dreams is to be an actress. Addison longs to be on the big screen and says that she would love a role in *Stranger Things*.

KEEP IT IN THE FAMILY

Addison isn't the only one in the house on TikTok – her whole family are at it! Her mum Sheri and her dad Monty both have profiles and her two little brothers, Lucas and Enzo, can be spotted on the family account.

ADDISON STATS

DOB: 6th October 2000
Star sign: Libra
From: Los Angeles, California, USA
TT style: Dancer
Full name: Addison Rae Easterling
Fave pop star: Billie Eilish
Fave place: The beach

@itsjojosiwa

JOJO SIWA

Somewhere over the rainbow-bow

Whether you're on top of your TikToks or not, you're probably well aware of JoJo Siwa and her trademark side ponytail. This little ray of sunshine is loud, proud and likely to be your little sister's favourite thing ever (even if she did get detention for wearing one of her over-sized hair bows to school.) JoJo has already had more successful careers than we've had slices of pizza (many, FYI) so it's no surprise that she's currently adding 'Top TikToker' to her CV.

TikTok
33.2m
followers

RISING STAR

JoJo's career began on popular dance shows *Abby's Ultimate Dance Competition* and *Dance Moms* in 2015 before she kick-ball-changed her way up the charts as a pop star.

PRETTY AS A PRESENT

She's never seen without a mahoosive hair bow which is probably why she has her own line of them at Claire's. How many does she have at home? About 800, apparently. Yikes!

JoJo looking cute at 12 years old.

CHART TOPPER

Not only has she released a load of top bops like *Boomerang* and *Kid In A Candy Store*, she was also revealed as the T-Rex on the US version of *The Masked Singer*.

I'M COMING OUT!

In Jan 2021, JoJo came out as a member of the LGBTQ+ community, saying she'd 'never felt happier.' She then went Insta-official with GF Kylie and the world exploded with love and rainbows.

JOJO STATS

DOB: 19th May 2003
Star sign: Taurus
From: Omaha, Nebraska, USA
TT style: Dancer and lip-syncer
Full name: Joelle Joanie Siwa
Pet: Yorkshire Terrier called Bow-Bow
Sibling: Big bro Jayden Siwa

TIKTOK'S
TOP 10 CHALLENGES

It's not an official top ten, before you start writing in to complain

Unless you've spent some time at the bottom of a well recently, you'll know that TikTok is full of these things called 'challenges'. And once a video of someone doing a certain dance routine, make-up look, lip-sync, outfit 'quick-change' (or anything really!) blows up, then everyone wants a slice of the viral pie. TikTokers around the world rise up to try it out themselves and thus a 'challenge' is born. Here are some you might have been tempted to have a go at ...

All hail @dallinxbella The original Flip the Switch creators

1

FLIP THE SWITCH

You've almost definitely seen this one. Two people – usually a couple – are dancing to Drake's song *Non Stop* when one of them flicks the light switch off. When the light flicks back on they've traded places, clothes and accessories ... like some kind of TikTok wizardry.

It's all about the editing ... and roping in your family!

2 WIPE IT DOWN

In this one, TikTokers are seen wiping down a mirror with a cleaning spray and on the fourth 'swipe' they appear in an alternate reality. Set to the tune *Wipe It Down* by BMW Kenny, this challenge has seen a rise in teenagers actually cleaning stuff – and no doubt a rise in mums rejoicing.

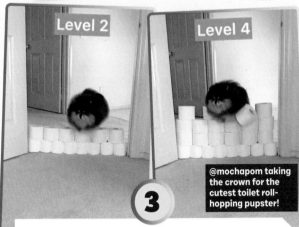

Level 2

Level 4

@mochapom taking the crown for the cutest toilet roll-hopping pupster!

3 LEVEL UP

Build a wall with toilet paper and then film yourself – or even better, a dog – jumping over the stack. With every successful jump, add another layer of loo roll and repeat until you, or your dog, fails. Set to Ciara's *Level Up*, we recommend roping in the cutest pupper you can find.

4 PLANK CHALLENGE

Oh, the plank. It's right up there with the burpee as one of the most hellish bits of a workout. So why people started a planking challenge we'll never know. To complete, hold a plank next to a pal and then do various different tricky positions without collapsing.

You might be able to plank, but that twin synchronicity is the stuff of TikTok dreams.

Couples get extra likes, especially in a fitness challenge. Goals!

Blink and you'll miss it, as shown by @jadethirlwall.

7 FLOUR CHALLENGE

A great one if you have annoying friends or siblings. Sit two of them down in front of a bowl of flour. Then answer some simple questions, for example 'which is the messiest?', by dunking their faces into the flour. Simple, fun, but a pain to clear up.

5 SHOE FLIP TRANSITION

One of the most popular and effective challenges. TikTokers are seen sitting and lip-syncing to *XIX* by Kismet when they drop a shoe onto their foot and BAM! All of a sudden, their entire outfit has changed, which could save a *lot* of time in the morning.

Showing off your creativity is at the heart of all TikToks!

Great for pranking TikTok families, as you can see ...

Gotta love a flour-dunking mum on the Tok!

6 BLINDING LIGHTS

As the challenge name suggests, this is all about The Weeknd's massive 2020 tune *Blinding Lights*. Unlike most other dance challenges there's no set choreography, TikTok users just make up their own routine, often inspired by the tune's eighties vibe.

In case you needed proof that this one is for gymnasts.

8

STAND UP

This one is nearly impossible, unless you're some sort of super gymnast. Two people are needed: the first lies on their stomach with the other stood on their back. The person on the ground gradually stands up with the other person hopping up too, until they're doing a very difficult-looking shoulder stand.

Always end your TikToks with awesome iconic finishing moves.

9

STAIR SHUFFLE

This is pretty much what it sounds like ... 'shuffling up a flight of stairs' usually set to *Pretty Girl* by Maggie Lindemann. Little Mix's Perrie Edwards and her boyfriend Liverpool footballer Alex Oxlade-Chamberlain gave it a go, making it look easy-peasy. Which we're pretty sure it's not.

BEAUTIFUL PEOPLE

You all know the song ... and probably partly because of this challenge. TikTokers all over the world started uploading videos of their beautiful people in their lives. And it was all just so ... what is the word ... beautiful! We're not crying, *you're* crying!

Some days it's just great to be kind to your mum!

@dixiedamelio

DIXIE D'AMELIO

They said it was a family affair ... they weren't lying

That unusual surname rings a bell, doesn't it? We'll tell you why it's familiar – it's because Dixie here is the older sister of TikTok top Toker, Charli D'Amelio. After her lookalike little sis started posting videos on the platform, Dixie followed in her footsteps and has become almost as popular. Not quite though. That must cause some friction around the dinner table.

TikTok
42.3m
followers

WHEELY BIG STAR

It seems that she was always destined for big things, in one way or another. When she was much younger she used to race BMX bikes and was 'fifth in the nation.'

Dixie's down-to-earth attitude sets her apart on the Tok.

NAUGHTY BUT NICE

Having released her debut single *Happy* in June 2020, Dixie later recorded a Christmas song with One Direction star, Liam Payne. *Naughty List.* It's unconfirmed if she received anything other than coal in her stocking.

HIGH FLYER

Dixie dated fellow TikTok star Griffin Johnson for about four months in 2020. On their last date, Griffin hired a helicopter to take her to dinner but they broke up soon after, proving that money can't buy love.

MODEL SISTER

As well as acting and singing, Dixie can also add 'model' to her CV. According to her dad, her first paid modelling gig was at the start of 2018 and since then she's worked with big-hitting brands like Ralph Lauren.

DIXIE STATS

DOB: 12th August 2001
Star sign: Leo
From: Norwalk, Connecticut, USA
TT style: Dancer and lip-syncher
Middle name: Jane
Fave film: *The Cat In The Hat*
Height: Approx 5'6"

@maxandharveyofficial

MAX AND HARVEY

Because two is better than one, after all

No, you don't need to book an eye test. We promise you're not seeing double. Max and Harvey are in fact identical twins which means they're the same age, same star sign and look so similar that when they were younger they used to do that typical twin prank and pretend to be each other in class. In all honesty, we're still not entirely sure which is which, although apparently Max is more likely to wear a hat.

TikTok
6m
followers

THE FAME GAME

Max and Harvey began singing when they were about eight years old and did some musical theatre in the West End before joining musical.ly in 2016. The rest, as they say, is history.

Different lab coats are essential items when you share an identical look.

Lead guitarist and a lead singer in one!

FAMILY TIES

The boys say that dad Paul is their biggest influence. Paul was also a singer, mainly in West End musicals, and met their mum Sara while performing on a cruise ship.

HEY BABY!

When identical twins are born, one has to come out before the other. That's just a biological fact. And with these brothers it was Harvey, making his entrance into the world two whole minutes before Max.

THE X FACTOR

The brothers competed on *The X Factor: Celebrity* in the summer of 2019, and came second place behind show-winner reality star Megan McKenna.

MAX AND HARVEY STATS

DOB: 31st December 2002
Star sign: Capricorn
From: Frimley, Surrey, UK
TT style: Singing and comedy
Inspirations: Shawn Mendes and Bruno Mars
Siblings: Younger brother Leo and sister Tilly
Max's guilty pleasure: Bacon bits
Harvey's fave pastime: Doing magic

20
TIKTOK TUNES
to stream now

Pop on a playlist and pretend you're Addison Rae

1

LAXED (SIREN BEAT) by Jawsh 685
Don't know the words? Don't worry, there aren't any.

2

ROSES (IMANBEK REMIX) by Saint Jhn & J Balvin
Hips and hands at the ready? Alrighty then.

3

SAY SO by Doja Cat
This one's more viral than the common cold. And it keeps spreading further!

4

BEAUTIFUL PEOPLE by Ed Sheeran
Think of your faves and feel the love.

5

BLINDING LIGHTS by The Weeknd
Get your fancy footwork ready, steady, go!

6

PRETTY GIRL by Maggie Lindemann
Here's a dusty one from the musical.ly archives.

7

OLD TOWN ROAD by Lil Nas X
Not a tune until TikTok took it to the Billboard lists!

8

SUPALONELY by Benee feat. Gus Dapperton
Altogether now – *La La La La Lonely!*

9

ROXANNE
by Arizona Zervas
Roxanne sounds like our kinda girl, tbh. Tuneeee.

10

STUNNIN'
by Curtis Waters feat. Harm Franklin
You really are. Now walk us through your wardrobe.

11

DANCE MONKEY
by Tones and I
Not sure what a dance monkey is, but we want one.

12

DEATH BED (COFFEE FOR YOUR HEAD)
by Powfu feat. Beabadoobee
Two sugars please.

13

COINCIDANCE
by Handsome Dancer
Stroke your ego and show us yer moves.

14

VIBE (IF I BACK IT UP)
by Cookiee Kawaii
Get ready for some serious shaking.

15

LOTTERY (RENEGADE)
by K Camp
Just don't knock yourself out with the punchy beat.

16

BORED IN THE HOUSE by Tyga feat. Curtis Roach
Basically the soundtrack to everyone's 2020.

17

NONSTOP
by Drake
Don't get caught in a trouser leg when flipping the switch.

18

BACKYARD BOY
by Claire Rosinkranz & Jeremy Zucker
Shut your eyes and dream of summer.

19

MOTION SICKNESS by Phoebe Bridgers
A dry ginger biscuit might help with that.

20

WHAT YOU KNOW BOUT LOVE
by Pop Smoke
Get ready to do your best slomo walk.

TIKTOK'S TOP

Or just tip top editing skills? Who can tell?

EVAN THE CARD GUY
@thecardguy

TikTok **16.2m** followers

Evan doesn't just do card tricks he also quizzes friends, family and other TikTok magicians with puzzles and riddles. He started doing magic aged 12 when his parents grounded him for playing too many video games!

TikTok **52.6m** followers

ZACH KING
@zachking

Zach doesn't claim to be a 'magician' and admits that his world famous illusions (riding a hover board, turning people into Selena Gomez, so many more) are more often than not the result of hours of editing. King by name, illusion king by nature.

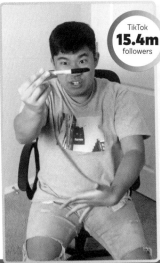
TikTok **15.4m** followers

SEAN DOES MAGIC
@seandoesmagic

Sean Sotaridona is still pretty young compared to all the other TikTok tricksters but that doesn't mean he can't pull a crowd with his funny, interactive magic. Plus he often reveals the secrets other magicians keep under their top hats.

TRICKSTERS

● ● ● ●

TikTok 3.9m followers

Look at your hand!

JACKSON ACES

@jacksonaces

Keep your thoughts to yourself if Jackson is around, because he's one of the best mind readers around. Jackson is from Sydney, Australia and started doing tricks when his mum bought him some cards for his 12th birthday present.

TikTok 881k followers

MAGIC SINGH

@magicsingh

London's Amardeep Singh Dhanjal started practising card tricks when he was a kid, desperate to wow his friends in the playground. He's now wowing 2m TikTok followers with next level card tricks and sleight of hand wizardry.

TikTok 2m followers

PATRICK KUN

@patrickkun

Thailand's Patrick Kun has some serious sleight of hand skills which is why his fanbase is growing. He's already got a line of merchandise! As well as clever card and coin tricks he can change the shape of things that you're looking at in the mirror.

37

@babyariel

BABY ARIEL

Not under the sea, that's the other one

Why Ariel refers to herself as a baby we're not sure as the last time we checked, there wasn't one real life baby who has a string of music videos, a couple of Teen Choice awards and their own anti-bullying campaign tucked in their nappy. So she's probably not *really* a baby, she's probably a super successful creator who has been around since the musical.ly days.

TikTok
34.8m
followers

BIG IN JAPAN

Ariel loves singing and has released eight of her own music singles. Her first, *Aww*, released in 2017, reached number 10 on Billboard Japan.

BIG EVERYWHERE ELSE TOO

Also in 2017, she was recognised as one of the most influential people on the internet by *Time* magazine and took home the Teen Choice award for 'Choice Muser' two years running.

DESTINATION, ZOMBIETOWN

Watch out when there's a full moon as she's also a part-time werewolf. Baby Ariel plays Wynter, a member of the Forbidden Forest's werewolf pack in the Disney Channel's *Zombies 2*. Awoo!

FUN AND (EA) GAMES

If you're wondering what she'd look like as a Sims character, she's got that covered. Ariel collaborated with EA Games, appearing as a Sim in the expansion pack *The Sims 4: Get Famous*.

ARIEL STATS

DOB: 22nd November 2000
Star sign: Scorpio
From: Pembroke Pines, Florida, USA
TT style: Singing and lip-syncing
Full name: Ariel Rebecca Martin
Fave colour: Red
Siblings: One brother, Jacob

@jacobsartorius

JACOB SARTORIUS

Your favourite ear wiggling social media megastar

TikTok
23.7m
followers

If TikTok was a school disco, then baby-faced Jacob Sartorius would be the first to show up, the first – and possibly the last – on the dance floor, and the one you'd most likely want to snog. Back when TikTok was musical.ly, he was straight in there with the funny videos and lip-syncing, establishing himself as one of the most successful creators of all time. And here he is, still nailing the videos.

A GOOD START

The first video Jacob uploaded to Vine in 2014 was a message about anti-bullying which ended up going viral and kick-starting his social media career.

The energy of a boy who just stood up to the bullies.

BOP TO IT

The creator has a fair few bops under his belt including his major label debut *Left Me Hangin'*, *Better With You* and the cute Christmas song, *Cozy*. He even toured with The Vamps.

LOVE IS STRANGE

Jacob has a rather famous ex-girlfriend: Millie Bobby Brown who plays Eleven in the show *Stranger Things*. The pair dated for about six months in 2017 before a demogorgan ran off with their love and buried it somewhere in Hawkins*.

(*unconfirmed.)

SECOND NATURE

It seems as though music is in his veins. He began singing and performing when he was just eight years old, started learning the guitar when he was 12 and can even tinkle some tunes on the piano.

JACOB STATS

DOB: 2nd October 2002
Star sign: Libra
From: Reston, Virginia, USA
TT style: Singer and comedian
Real name: Rolf. Jacob is his middle name!
Party trick: Wiggling his ears
Fave drink: Chocolate milk

41

HOW TO
TALK TIKTOK

Because cracking out a 'hun' is so yesterday, bae

EXTRA

Urban dictionary definition: Over the top, excessive, dramatic behaviour.

Take it to the Tok: *"Apparently she painted her cat's nails to match her own! She's so extra."*

FIRE

Urban dictionary definition: Something really good, amazing and crazy in a good way.

Total FIRE

Take it to the Tok: *"Zach's new magic trick is total fire."*

FLEX

Urban dictionary definition: To purposely brag or show off something you have.

Take it to the Tok: *"Did you notice her mum drop her off in their new sports car? Cool flex."*

COOL FLEX!

GOALS

Urban dictionary definition: What people say to each other when someone posts a pic that is very attractive or is of something they aspire to, like a relationship.

Take it to the Tok: *"Brooklyn Beckham and Nicola Peltz are total couple goals."*

HUNDO P

Urban dictionary definition: One hundred percent sure about something.

HUNDO P!

Take it to the Tok: *"Do I want to come to your sleepover? Hundo P!"*

KAREN

Urban dictionary definition: A bit of a mean term used for a woman perceived as entitled or demanding beyond what is appropriate or necessary.

Take it to the Tok: *"Mum is forever complaining about how messy my room is. She's such a Karen."*

SAVAGE

Urban dictionary definition:
Someone who isn't scared of anyone or anything and doesn't hold back their fire comebacks.

Take it to the Tok: "My brother ate the last slice of pizza. He's savage!"

SHOOK

Urban dictionary definition:
Shocked or surprised.

Take it to the Tok:
"When I heard about Dixie and Griffin splitting up, I was shook!"

SIMP

Urban dictionary definition:
Someone who does way too much for someone they like.

Take it to the Tok: "I can't believe you did his homework for him. You're such a simp!"

SNACK

Urban dictionary definition:
Someone who looks really hot.

Take it to the Tok:
"Have you seen that new boy in Year 9? He's a total snack."

SNATCHED

Urban dictionary definition:
Very attractive, flawlessly styled.

Take it to the Tok: "Did you see Charli D'Amelio in her new video? She's looking snatched."

SPOOPY

Urban dictionary definition:
Something that is funny and spooky at the same time.

Take it to the Tok: "Check out the cockapoo dressed up as a ghost for Halloween. He's so spoopy!"

STAN

Urban dictionary definition:
Based on the character in the Eminem song, a 'stan' is an overzealous maniacal fan for any celebrity.

Take it to the Tok: "I totally stan Shawn Mendes. He's the best."

TEA

Urban dictionary definition: The best kind of gossip, typically shared between friends. Usually about someone you know, but can extend to celebs and internet scandals.

Take it to the Tok: "Come on, spill the tea on that boy you fancy!"

YEET

Urban dictionary definition:
To discard an item at high speed.

Take it to the Tok: [Throwing your chicken nugget box into the bin] "Yeeeet!"

WHERE IN THE WORLD?

Because not all top TikTokers are from America

TikTok is popular (and that's an understatement). Around 800 million people use it worldwide. That's more than double the amount of people that live in the whole of America which is, quite frankly, an eye-popping, mind-boggling, nose-twisting amount. You might *think* that you already follow all of the popular creators on the app – and you might also think that the big players are all in the USA but with TikTok available in over 154 countries it makes sense that there's top Tokers in other countries too. So say Konnichiwa and G'day to this lot.

CANADA
- Wig fan **Kristen Hancher** was born in Ontario.

AMERICA
- **Charli** and **Dixie D'Amelio** were born in Norwalk, Connecticut.
- **Addison Rae** moved from hometown Louisiana to Los Angeles.
- There was magic in Portland, Oregon when **Zach King** was born.
- **Loren Gray** is originally from Pottstown, Pennsylvania.
- **Jacob Sartorius** was born in Oklahoma.
- **Avani Gregg** put Indiana on the map.

ARUBA
- Funny guys **Gilmher** and **Jayden Croes** grew up in Aruba's capital, Oranjestad.

AVANI GREGG

UK
● Funny girl **Amelia Gething** is London born and bred.
● Singing twins **Max and Harvey** are from Surrey.

MAX AND HARVEY

TURKEY
● Top TikTok chef **Burak Özdemir** is from Yayladağı.

JAPAN
● **Hina Yoshihara** is the Charli D'Amelio of Niiza, Saitama.

HINA YOSHIHARA

KOREA
● It's all dance and dogs from **Shana** who is Korea's most popular creator.

INDIA
● Cool kid **Riyaz Afreen** is from Jaigaon, Bhutan.
● Lip-syncing and LOLs from **Arishfa Khan** who started life in Shajahanpur.
● Jalhandar gave us actress and top TikToker **Avneet Kaur**.

AUSTRALIA
● Brisbane TikToker **Sarah Magusara** nails the latest dance moves.
● Northern Territory-born **Rory Eliza** quit school to pursue TikTok.

NEW ZEALAND
● Indian **Kishan** and American **Shanell** are New Zealand's most popular TikToking couple.

@sofiawylie

SOFIA WYLIE

Is there anything this girl can't do?

Sofia puts our CVs to shame. While the rest of us were still focusing on passing our GCSEs, she'd already entered numerous TV talent shows, had her first major acting role, started her own IGTV dance lessons and released a single. All while finding the time to become a major TikTok star. We need a little lie down just thinking about it ...

TikTok
8.2m
followers

PLACE THAT FACE

If her face is familiar it might be because you've seen it in the Disney Channel series *Andi Mack*. She plays high school student and basketball captain Buffy Driscoll.

Sofia with her *Andi Mack* co-stars.

SHE'S GOT PURPOSE

She kick-ball-changed her career in dance (you may have spotted her on *America's Got Talent* in 2015) but – green-eyed monster alert – she also danced on Justin Bieber's *Purpose* world tour.

WILDCAT AT HEART

When she was five she was flown to LA to attend the premiere of *High School Musical 3* after winning tickets in a competition. Ten years later she plays Gina in *High School Musical: The Musical: The Series*, which is like some serious cosmic ordering.

● ● ● ●

PUPPY LOVE

Sofia's dog Baby Violet is a star in her own right. The pupper has her own Instagram account with more than 4,000 followers where she wears sweaters and hangs out in handbags.

SOFIA STATS

DOB: 7th January 2004
Star sign: Capricorn
From: Tramonto, North Phoenix, USA
TT style: Dancing and lip-syncing
Siblings: Older sister Isabella
Pet: Yorkshire Terrier called Baby Violet
Celeb inspiration: Zendaya

@twitchtok7

STEPHEN 'TWITCH' BOSS

He'll dance like everyone's watching

I t's not every day that you come across someone as crushingly cool as Stephen 'tWitch' Boss. Unless you follow him on TikTok and then it's likely that you *do* actually come across him every day. Because, you know, he's on it nearly every day. Go and have a look. There he is again, dancing up a hip hop storm. When he's not acting in *Magic Mike XXL* and stuff like that.

TikTok
3.4m
followers

HEY, MR DJ

As well as acting and dancing, he's currently the resident DJ on the Ellen DeGeneres show and has been spinning records for the chat show queen since 2014.

TOUGH CHOICE

When asked whether he prefers dancing or acting, Stephen says it's almost impossible to answer as both are 'mediums of performance' and 'performing' is what he's most passionate about.

TWITCH, PLEASE!

Apparently there's two reasons for the 'tWitch' moniker. The first is that he was always 'popping and ticking' as a kid, so 'twitch' became a nickname. Secondly, he says it was the name of his old Toyota Paseo that he used to travel and choreograph in.

GROOVE IS IN THE HEART

You know Allison Holker? The professional dancer from *Dancing With The Stars*? She's married to Stephen which must be very nice for her. (He and his groomsmen wore fun shirts under their wedding jackets. Stephen was Superman, natch.)

TWITCH STATS

DOB: 29th September 1982
Star sign: Libra
From: Montgomery, Alabama, USA
TT style: Freestyle hip-hop dance
Children: Weslie, Maddox and Zaia
Pet: Jack Russell called Krypto
Fave superhero: Superman

You know-you were
BORN TO TIKTOK
when ...

YOU CAN'T HEAR A SONG WITHOUT LIP-SYNCING IT IN THE MIRROR

Your boyfriend gets pranked more than he gets hugged

Your attention span is roughly ... sorry, what?

You spend four hours on your make-up, then remove it after five minutes

YOUR FRIENDS SEE MORE OF YOU ON YOUR FEED THAN IRL

YOU'RE HAPPY FOR YOUR LITTLE BROTHER TO PRETEND TO PULL YOUR HEAD OFF

YOU'RE SAVING YOUR POCKET MONEY TO CHANGE YOUR SURNAME TO D'AMELIO

YOUR RINGTONE IS LAXED (SIREN BEAT)... ...AND YOU DO THE ROUTINE EVERY TIME SOMEONE CALLS

Your friends aren't your 'friends' they're your 'squad'. And you're total #squadgoals

You refer to opening a can of tuna as 'a challenge'

You're stockpiling loo roll ... for your dog to jump over

YOU CAN'T PUT SUNGLASSES ON WITHOUT SHOUTING 'DROP'

You think of your family as extras in the show of your life

You can't wait to get your hands on your mum's cleaning products

You jump your way to the school bus in time to *Where Is The Love?*

YOUR BEDROOM IS USED FOR CHALLENGES MORE THAN IT IS FOR SLEEPING

Whenever you wrap your hair in a towel you break into Mamma Mia

TOP TIKTOK

We went down a rabbit hole. Didn't find any rabbits ...

SHAQ
@shaqthepug
This little guy is just a normal pug living his best life in New York – and we are here for it. He's got a penchant for fancy dress and puppaccinos and can also fart out Halloween treats and cookies, which may or may not be down to some clever editing.

TikTok
4.4m
followers

TikTok
6.8m
followers

MOCHA
@mochapom
Have you ever seen a more fabulous ball of fluff? Mocha is a floofy, goofy Pomeranian who chooses her own outfits, has regular baths (with rose petals – told you she was fancy) and will steal your heart without thinking twice about it.

TikTok
552k
followers

A BUNCH OF DUCKS
@dunkin.ducks
There we were, begging dad for a dog all these years, and we should have tried asking for a duck (although maybe the bill would have been bigger ...). These cute, funny fellas wear harnesses to go on walks and take baths in fruit juice to dye them temporarily pink.

PET PICKS

TikTok
9.8m
followers

A COUPLE OF FERRETS
@friendlyquest

If you want to see ferrets taking on the TikTok dancing challenges – with a couple of guinea pigs thrown in for good measure – this profile is the place for you. Cute, funny, and cute again – which is exactly how we like our pawsome pet content.

TikTok
1.9m
followers

HUXLEY
@huxleythepandapuppy

A dog that looks like a panda and spends more of his time in fancy dress than out of it ... ? We're in ... Everyone is in! Plus, for a pup with such little legs we're extremely impressed that he can jump four layers of the Level Up challenge.

TikTok
5.5m
followers

MR. POTATO
@coolestpotatoe

Put your hands up if you're the sort of person who finds a cat miaowing along to Harry Styles' *Watermelon Sugar* beyond hilarious. Now put your hands down and scroll through TikTok until you find this beautiful ginger fellow.

@ameliagething

AMELIA GETHING

Let's Geth ready to rumble!

We know what you're thinking: all of those hugely successful TikTok creators are far, far away making videos in their bedrooms in other countries, right? Wrong! Enter Amelia Gething who was born and bred – and as far as we know, has her bedroom – in London. She uses TikTok to be hilarious and when the BBC came across her content they gave her her own show called *The Amelia Gething Complex* on CBBC.

TikTok
7.2m
followers

JUST FOR LOLS

Amelia started doing comedy skits on TikTok (when it was musical.ly) purely for LOLs and couldn't believe how many people found her funny.

One of Amelia's many characters

LAUGH OUT PROUD

One of the main reasons Amelia loves doing comedy is to show that women *can* be funny and says she finds it 'frustrating' when people assume only men can get a laugh.

DREAMING BIG

Despite being a huge TikTok creator and having her own successful CBBC show, Amelia's main goal is to be a full-time actress, staring in telly shows and films. So watch this space! (Well, not *this* space. Maybe the TV and film listings would be more helpful.)

THE FAMILY BUSINESS

It's no wonder that Amelia was set for stardom; her grandad is in a band and dresses up as the Grim Reaper while playing the banjo on stage.

AMELIA STATS

DOB: 24th January 1999
Star sign: Aquarius
From: London, UK
TT style: Comedy
Celeb lookalike: Anne Hathaway
Fave film: *Bridesmaids*
Comedy Inspiration: *The Mighty Boosh* and *Monty Python*

(@joshrichards)

JOSH RICHARDS

Mirror, mirror on TikTok's wall, who's the fairest of them all?

If TikTok were to choose a poster boy (and thinking about it, how we wish they would) they'd find it hard to choose anyone better for the job than Josh Richards. He sings, dances, lip-syncs and is a super-goof. Plus – and not that this matters to us at all – he's extremely easy on the eye. Is it any wonder the Canadian now lives in a TikTok mansion of the world's top Tokers? (The answer's no.)

TikTok
23.4m
followers

EX APPEAL

He had a high profile TikTok relationship with influencer Nessa Barrett. Fans referred to them as their 'smooshed' name 'Jessa' and when they split they posted a video to YouTube together saying they'd always be there for each other. No, *you're* crying.

RIP Jessa.

ACTING UP

As well as being big on the TikTok scene, Josh is also a bit of a star of the silver screen. His IMDB page lists movies *Summertime Dropouts*, *Brother's Keepers* and *Cardinal Sin* as films he's worked on. Someone grab the popcorn!

PRINCE CHARMING

According to talent bigwigs, Josh is set for superstardom. Michael Gruen, the Vice President of TalentX Entertainment, says there's no one more 'charming and charismatic' than Josh – and he's seen every TikToker in the world.

LET US SWAY

Josh is a member of 'Sway House' – a group of popular TikTok lads which includes Bryce Hall (above), Griffin Johnson and Anthony Reeves. The boys all live together in LA so we can only imagine what that place smells like.

JOSH STATS

DOB: 31st January 2002
Star sign: Aquarius
From: Toronto, Ontario, Canada
TT style: Lip-syncing and goofy skits
Siblings: Sister Olivia and brother William
Celeb crush: Selena Gomez
Fave actor: Will Smith

13 LESSER-KNOWN
TIKTOK TITBITS

If you know these facts about TikTok already, you probably should have written this book

1

Jacob Sartorius can only date girls who like chocolate milk. He's obsessed with the stuff so considers it a bit of a deal-breaker.

2

CHARLI AND DIXIE D'AMELIO'S DAD MARC RAN FOR CONNECTICUT STATE SENATE IN 2018 AS A REPUBLICAN.

4

Loren Gray's Pomeranian Smudge has her own Instagram page, @smudgeepom.

5

Creator Kristen Hancher suffered with scoliosis growing up and had to have her back straightened with steel rods screwed to her spine.

3

Stephen 'tWitch' Boss had to be 'waxed from head to toe' for his role in *Magic Mike*. He had his first wax live on the Ellen DeGeneres show.

6

Addison Rae is the first TikToker to land a major film role. She's due to play the lead character in *He's All That*, a remake of popular 90s romcom *She's All That*.

7

When he was a kid, Zach King wanted to be a magician and practised magic tricks with his grandpa from the age of 8.

8

JoJo Siwa once babysat for Kim Kardashian's kid North West! We need someone to keep an eye on us next weekend JoJo, just saying.

9

Max and Harvey's first taste of fame was when they were toddlers and alternatively played the role of Thomas in a drama show called *William and Mary*.

10

BABY ARIEL'S FIRST TATTOO WAS A BUTTERFLY ON HER WRIST THAT SHE GOT ON HER 19th BIRTHDAY.

11

As part of a prank on his best friend Jason Nash, creator David Dobrik married Jason's mum Lorraine in Vegas. They stayed married for six months before getting a divorce.

12

Amelia Gething loves The 1975 but says she's also obsessed with Ed Sheeran's music.

13

Astronauts can't cry in space, because of gravity. Nothing to do with TikTok, but interesting right?

20 MORE

TIKTOK BOPS
to pop on a playlist

It's like the world's longest dance party, isn't it?

1

RENEE
by Sales
Get ready for some of that life-affirming good stuff.

2

BOSS BITCH
by Doja Cat
Ready to feel super pumped? You da boss.

3

THE BOX
by Roddy Rich
Mum will be pleased to see you with cleaning products.

4

LALALA
by Y2K & Bbno$
It's like Rock, Paper, Scissors but with emojis.

5

CANNIBAL
by Kesha
Wash your hands before using fingers to stir tea, kids.

6

BANANA
by Conkarah (feat. Shaggy) – Minisiren Remix
Sunglasses on forehead? Drop!

7

LEVEL UP
by Ciara
Well, how many loo rolls can your dog jump?

8

DON'T RUSH by Young T & Bugsey feat Headie One
Make-up brushes at the ready for the big reveal.

9

SOBER UP
by AJR feat.
Rivers Cuomo
Hello, hello!
Where *are* you
supposed to be?

10

M TO THE B
by Millie B
Go easy on the
head bobbing,
now.

11

LET'S LINK
by WhoHeem
We don't
condone
cheating, tho.

12

FAMOUS
(I'M THE ONE)
by Mozzy
All this clothes
swapping is
getting a bit chilly.

13

OK KLAHOMA
by Jack Stauber
White sheets at
the ready? Let's
get spooky!

14

ATTENTION
by Todrick Hall
Oi! Over here!
Do we have your
attention?

15

HIT THA ROOF
by Speed Gang
Maybe use a box
if you can't quite
reach the roof.

16

PSYCHO!
by Masn
Would it help if
you took a few
deep breaths?

17

LOSE CONTROL
by Meduza &
Becky Hill &
Goodboys
Another dance to
learn? Sure.

18

TOOSIE SLIDE
by Drake
Ready? Right
foot up, left
foot slide ...

19

I LIKE HIM
by Princess
Nokia
Play nice now
please, ladies.

20

ANGEL EYES
from Mama
Mia Movie
Soundtrack
The perfect one
for post hair wash.

ARE YOU
ON TOP OF TIKTOK?

Here's where we see who's been paying attention ...

1 **What was TikTok called before it became TikTok?**
- A) music.fans
- B) musical.ly
- C) musical.ity
- D) music.makers

2 **Charli D'Amelio stole the 'most popular creator' crown from ... who?**
- A) Jacob Sartorius
- B) Addison Rae
- C) Zach King
- D) Loren Gray

3 **What is the name of Sofia Wylie's Insta-famous pupper?**
- A) Baby Violet
- B) Baby Ariel
- C) Baby Cakes
- D) Baby Belle

4 **Where did Max and Harvey's dad Paul meet their mum Sara?**
- A) At a West End theatre
- B) On a cruise ship
- C) In a supermarket's pet food aisle
- D) On an internet dating site

5 **'Spilling the tea' means ...**
- A) Something so funny, you spit your tea out
- B) The hot beverage drinking challenge
- C) Sharing gossip with friends
- D) Predicting the future

MAX AND HARVEY

6 If you 'stan' someone you …
A) Can't stand them
B) Are obsessed with them
C) Want to be them
D) Are in competition with them

7 Which creator took Dixie D'Amelio on a helicopter date?
A) Gilmher Coes
B) Alex Stokes
C) Jacob Sartorius
D) Griffin Johnson

8 Where did Stephen 'tWitch' Boss get his nickname?
A) His car
B) His nan
C) His love for witches
D) His first album

9 In 2019 a Zach King video became the most viewed TikTok. What was he doing?
A) Making orange juice
B) A clever card trick
C) Flying a broomstick
D) Bringing a polar bear to life

10 Which actress did Jacob Sartorius famously date?
A) Millie Bobby Brown
B) Sophia Lillis
C) Sophia Grace
D) Madison Bailey

ANSWERS
1 B, 2 D, 3 A, 4 B, 5 C,
6 B, 7 D, 8 A, 9 C, 10 A

8 - 10

TOP TOK-ER
You've been reading this book in your sleep again, haven't you? Either that or you're totally and utterly obsessed. Go straight to the top of the TikTok class!

4 - 7

CAUGHT IN THE MIDDLE
Top Tok marks for your effort. You certainly know more than most but, if push came to shove, could you tell the difference between Max and Harvey? Well, could you?

1 - 3

TIC-FLOP
Hello? Have you even heard of the global phenomenon that is TikTok? No, we didn't think so. Go back and read this book again before we get totally savage with you.

CHARLI D'AMELIO

STEPHEN 'TWITCH' BOSS

CREDITS

Cover: Getty Images/Stephane Cardinale - Corbis, Getty Images/David Becker, Getty Images/Emma McIntyre, Getty Images/Leon Bennett, Getty Images/NBC, Getty Images/Jim Spellman, Getty Images/Frederick M. Brown.

04-05: Getty Images/Jeff Spicer, Getty Images/Gregg DeGuire, Abaca Press/Alamy Images, Getty Images/David Becker, Getty Images/Andreas Rentz/MTV 2018,Getty Images/Gregg DeGuire, Getty Images/Tasia Wells, Getty Images/Dimitrios Kambouris, Getty Images/Aaron J. Thornton, Getty Images/Gregg DeGuire, Getty Images/Michael Loccisano, Getty Images/Jon Kopaloff.

06-07: Words: BBC Bitzesize

08-09: Getty Images/Laura Cavanaugh, Getty Images/Paul Zimmerman, Getty Images/Gregg DeGuire, Getty Images/Taylor Hill.

10-11: TikTok/@creatorgirll, TikTok/@ashleighquiroz, TikTok/caseyc0w, TikTok/demibagby, TikTok/omsteve.

12-13: Getty Images/Jon Kopaloff, Getty Images/Vivien Killileam, Getty Images/Tristar Media, Getty Images/Image Group LA, Getty Images/Gilbert Carrasquillo, Getty Images/Andreas Rentz/MTV 2018, Getty Images/David Livingston, Getty Images/JB Lacroix.

14-15: Instagram/@charlidamelio, TikTok/@charlidamelio, Getty Images/Alberto E. Rodriguez, Getty Images/Vittorio Zunino Celotto, Getty Images/Michael Loccisano.

16-17: Getty Images/CBS Photo Archive, Getty Images/Tara Ziemba, TikTok/@zachking, Getty Images/Gregg DeGuire.

18-19: Getty Images/Kevin Mazur, Getty Images/Young Hollywood, Getty Images/Charley Gallay.

20-21: TikTok/@zachking, TikTok/@charlidamelio, TikTok/@itsjojosiwa, TikTok/@mochapom.

22-23: Getty Images/Frazer Harrison, TikTok/@addisonre, Instagram/@addisonraee, Getty Images/David Livingston.

24-25: WENN Rights Ltd/Alamy Images, TikTok/@itsjojosiwa, Instagram/@itsjojosiwa, Image Press Agency/Alamy Images.

26-27: TikTok/@dallinxbella, TikTok/@justmaiko, TikTok/@mochapom, TikTok/@stokestwins, TikTok/@jessbelkin.

28-29: TikTok/@jadethirlwall, TikTok/@daviddobrik, TikTok/@robbrizzlee, TikTok/@scott_mathison_, TikTok/@perrieedwards, TikTok/@katyhedges.

30-31: Instagram/@dixiedamelio, TikTok/@dixiedamelio, Instagram/@imgriffinjohnson, Getty Images/Michael Loccisano.

32-33: Instagram/@maxandharvey, TikTok/@maxandharveyofficial, Getty Images/Karwai Tang, Getty Images/Jeff Spicer.

34-35: 1 Columbia Records, 2 Hitco and Godd Complexx Inc, 3 Kemosabe Records/RCA Records, 4 Asylum Records UK, 5 The Weeknd XO Inc, 6 300 Entertainment, 7 Columbia Records, 8 Republic Records, 9 Arizona Zervas, 10 Curtis Waters Inc, 11 Bad Batch Records, 12 Columbia Records, 13 Handsome Dancer, 14 The Cookie Jar/Empire, 15 Rare Sound/Interscope/Empire, 16 Smile Anyways/LLC and Last Kings Records, 17 Young Money/Cash Money Records, 18 Purple Monkey Recordz LLC, 19 Dead Oceans, 20 Republic Records/Victor Victor Worldwide.

36-37: TikTok/@zachking, TikTok/@seandoesmagic, TikTok/@thecardguy, TikTok/@jacksonaces, TikTok/@magicsingh, TikTok/@patrickkun.

38-39: Getty Images/Presley Ann, TikTok/@babyariel, Instagram/@babyariel, Getty Images/Dominik Bindl, Getty Images/Michael Kovac.

40-41: Getty Images/NurPhoto, TikTok/@jacobsartorius, Getty Images/David M. Benett, Getty Images/Johnny Louis, Getty Images/David Becker.

44-45: Getty Images/Alberto E. Rodriguez, Image used under license from Shutterstock.com, Getty Images/Shirlaine Forrest, Getty Images/Mauricio Santana.

46-47: Getty Images/Mitch Haaseth, TikTok/@sofiawylie, Instagram/@sofiawylie, Getty Images/Leon Bennett.

48-49: Getty Images/NBC, TikTok/@twitchtok7, Getty Images/Charley Gallay, Getty Images/Matt Winkelmeyer.

52-53: TikTok/@mochapom, TikTok/@shaqthepug, TikTok/@dunkin.ducks, TikTok/@friendlyquest, TikTok/@huxleythepandapuppy, TikTok/@coolestpotatoe.

54-55: Instagram/@ameliagething, TikTok/@ameliagething, Getty Images/Stephane Cardinale - Corbis.

56-57: Instagram/@joshrichards, TikTok/@joshrichards, Getty Images/Bryan Steffy.

58-59: Getty Images/Steve Granitz, Instagram/@smudgepom, YouTube/Jojo Siwa Its TV, Getty Images/Daniele Venturelli.

60-61: 1 Sales, 2 Getty Images/Frazer Harrison, 3 WEA International Inc, 4 Y2K Music Inc and BBNO Music Inc, 5 RCA Records, 6 Conkarah, 7 Beauty Entertainment, 8 Black Butter Limited, 9 AJR Productions LLC, 10 B1 Records Limited, 11 WhoHeem, 12 Mozzy Records/Empire, 13 Plopscotch Records, 14 Todrick Hall, 15 Speed Gang, 16 RCA Records, 17 Meduza, 18 Ovo, 19 Princess Nokia, 20 Polydor Records/Littlestar Services Limited.

62-63: Getty Images/Jo Hale, Getty Images/Pietro S. D'Aprano, Getty Images/Steve Granitz.

Back cover: Getty Images/Pietro S. D'Aprano.